TAIL-LESS CATS & THREE-LEGGED MEN

THE ISLE OF MAN

Ian Moncrief-Scott

Information Management Solutions Limited

ISLE OF MAN

The author Ian Moncrief-Scott has asserted his right under the Copyright, Designs and Patents Act 1988 to be identified as the author of this work.

Copyright. © I. Moncrief-Scott 2021

All rights reserved. No part of this publication may be produced in any form or by any means - graphic, electronic, or mechanical, including photocopying, recording, taping, or information storage and retrieval systems - without the prior permission in writing of the publishers.

The publishers make no representation, express or implied, regarding the accuracy of the information contained in this book and cannot accept any legal responsibility for any errors or omissions that may take place.

A CIP catalogue record for this book is available from the British Library.

Published by Information Management Solutions Limited, 17 Howe Road, Onchan, Isle of Man, IM3 2BB.

Printed, bound and distributed by IngramSpark.

Book Layout © 2017 BookDesignTemplates.com

Superhero Peg Image: Besjunior/Shutterstock.com

Cover Source by Tanja Prokop of BookDesignTemplates.com

TAIL-LESS CATS & THREE-LEGGED MEN: THE ISLE OF MAN - 1st ed.
ISBN 99781903467091

The Publishers have been requested by the author to acknowledge the direct and indirect contributions to this book by the Isle of Man Government.

This book is dedicated to
start-up entrepreneurs.

The front cover depicts
ordinary wooden clothes pegs dressed as
Super Heroes.

**All start-up entrepreneurs are
ordinary people
turning into Super Heroes!**

CONTENTS

TAIL-LESS CATS & THREE-LEGGED MEN 1
OTHER BOOKS BY THE AUTHOR 5
FORTHCOMING BOOKS BY THE AUTHOR 7

TAIL-LESS CATS & THREE-LEGGED MEN

Becoming the globe's most prudential offshore centre has not been uneventful.

Though tail-less cats and three-legged men inspire mystique, the Isle of Man's financial history is an intriguing reality.

Deprived of intrinsic raw materials, but fortified by 'herrin and spuds' (sea fish and potatoes), Manxmen chose international trade for independent survival.

Manx ships carried the Pilgrim Fathers and helped break the American blockade!

For a time, the Isle was decried as a smugglers' haunt. In 1661 official records show 'a nest of smucklers who glory in their treasons.' Even the local Bishop, in 1742, declared 'the iniquitous trade will hinder the blessing of God from falling upon us.'

The Island had long been a magnet for foreign marauders. Norsemen first recognised the strategic importance for trading and harassing shipping. Adjacent kingdoms, England, Scotland, and Ireland all vied for control.

Now she was in conflict with her current master.

England had granted exclusive charters to companies exploiting her Colonies. The Crown applied taxes to imported goods at home and abroad, including tobacco, tea, silk, salt, wine, and spirits.

Manxmen spotted an opportunity. Provided local dues were met, these products could be re-sold abroad. They began importing, warehousing and re-exporting.

Outraged, the English Government screamed 'smugglers' and applied huge pressure on local officials to stamp out the evil. Manx leaders turned a blind eye. 'Mischief' prevailed.

By 1765, the year of the infamous Stamp Act that sparked the War of Independence, England's patience was exhausted. The Duke of Atholl was pressed to sell all fiscal rights for £70,000.

He did not consult the Manx. They were justifiably furious.

Perhaps, George Quayle, a relation of US Senator Dan Quayle, epitomises the period. Through his forebears' trading success with the Americas and the East, George had a comfortable start to life in 1751.

He soon became popular with local merchants but his family shunned his ambitions in common business. For generations, George's name would not be mentioned at dinner.

In 1802, backed by Major John Taubman, he launched the Island's first bank, The Isle of Man Banking Company. Quayle's notes quickly became known' as good as the Bank of England's.

He closed the bank in 1818. Worthy of standards demanded today, George sold personal property to fully refund depositors.

Many also believe he was an expert 'smuggler'. At Bridge House, in Castletown, now a Museum, his office resembles a stern cabin of Nelson's era. From the deck, with its panoramic view, George monitored traffic, especially the Revenue.

With a secret harbour tunnel, passageways and 'dumb waiters', cargo could be unobtrusively discharged from the dock beneath the building.

Quayle even had a swivelling fireplace concealing a safe. Hidden compartments in chart-lockers and cupboards kept vital documents from prying eyes. Complex locking mechanisms, operated by horsehair cables over remote pulleys, guarded his inconspicuous fortress.

With remarkable foresight, before he died in 1835, he walled-up his small sloop with records, documents, and equipment in her berth beneath the office. Warning his family that doom would descend on anyone who disturbed its fate, 'Peggy' remained in her silt coffin for 100 years until a workman fell through the floor.

Much important history was revealed, including secret plans for a huge barge to carry 30,000 troops for a Napoleonic invasion.

Today, Tynwald, the world's longest-serving continuous Government, steers a booming economy, sustaining independent growth through low, effective taxation.

Bolstered by Moody's and Standard & Poors AAA ratings, the Isle of Man is fully grasping the e-commerce revolution and using her three legs to still run rings around the opposition.

OTHER BOOKS BY THE AUTHOR

As Good As Gold - History of Pound Sterling. ISBN 0-9534818-4-0

De La Rue Straw Hats to Global Securities. ISBN 0- 9534818-2-4

Euro History & Development. ISBN 0-9534818-1-6

Holidays 2000 – A Time Capsule. ISBN 0-9534818-7-5

Negotiate to Win! - The Introductory Edition. ISBN 0-9534818-6-7

Start Any Business (Print). ISBN 9781903467008
Start Any Business (eBook). ISBN 9781903467015

Scripophily - Historic Bond & Share Collecting. ISBN 0-9534818-5-9

Tail-less Cats & Three-legged Men (eBook). ISBN 9781903467183

The Eternal Old Lady - Bank of England. ISBN 0-9534818-3-2

The Green Shoots of Money (Print). ISBN 9781903467107
The Green Shoots of Money (eBook). ISBN 9781903467114

The Hitmen - Part One. ISBN 0-9534818-8-3

FORTHCOMING BOOKS BY THE AUTHOR

As Good As Gold (Print). ISBN 9781903467039
As Good As Gold (eBook). ISBN 9781903467121

Currants, Olives & Cotton (Print). ISBN 9781903467077
Currants, Olives & Cotton (eBook). ISBN 9781903467169

De La Rue (Print). ISBN 9781903467046
De La Rue (eBook). ISBN 9781903467138

Euro (Print). ISBN 9781903467053
Euro (eBook). ISBN 9781903467145

Scripophily (Print). ISBN 9781903467084
Scripophily (eBook). ISBN 9781903467176

The Eternal Old Lady (Print). ISBN 9781903467060
The Eternal Old Lady (eBook). ISBN 9781903467152

ABOUT THE AUTHOR

Ian Moncrief-Scott has over fifty years of broad business experience, mostly gained at international level, based in the UK.

As a former senior executive for a global publishing and information technology company headquartered in the USA, he has contributed to numerous client-facing procurement and outsourcing initiatives worldwide.

Ian has created and participated in numerous small businesses in the UK, Isle of Man and elsewhere.

He has also represented the Isle of Man Government Department for Enterprise in several of its business support schemes. Ian designed and delivered extensive training for its Micro Business Grant Scheme.

In recognition of his long-term service to the Department, Ian was nominated for The Queen's Award for Enterprise Promotion and awarded an official Certificate of Recognition in 2018.

Throughout his career, he has maintained an active interest in start-ups, especially those involving the financial sector.

At the turn of the millennium, several of the articles written by Ian that form this short work were originally published by the Museum of American Financial History (now the Museum of American Finance).

www.ingramcontent.com/pod-product-compliance
Lightning Source LLC
Chambersburg PA
CBHW071722080526
44588CB00012B/1872